READABOUT

© 1992 Franklin Watts

Franklin Watts
96 Leonard Street
London EC2A 4RH

Franklin Watts Australia
14 Mars Road
Lane Cove
NSW 2066

UK ISBN: 0 7496 0858 7

A CIP catalogue record for this book
is available from the British Library

Editor: Ambreen Husain
Design: K and Co

Typesetting: Lineage Ltd, Watford, England
Printed in Hong Kong

Additional photographs:
Frank Spooner Pictures (Alexis Duclos) p31.

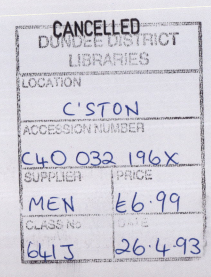

READABOUT

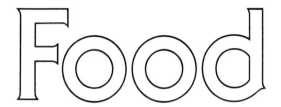
Food

Text: Henry Pluckrose
Photography: Chris Fairclough

Franklin Watts
London/New York/Sydney/Toronto

Human beings need food.
Our body uses the food
we eat in several ways.
Food provides us with energy.

Food also contains
the vitamins and proteins
our bodies need
to grow and stay healthy.

When babies are first born they are fed on milk made in their mother's body.

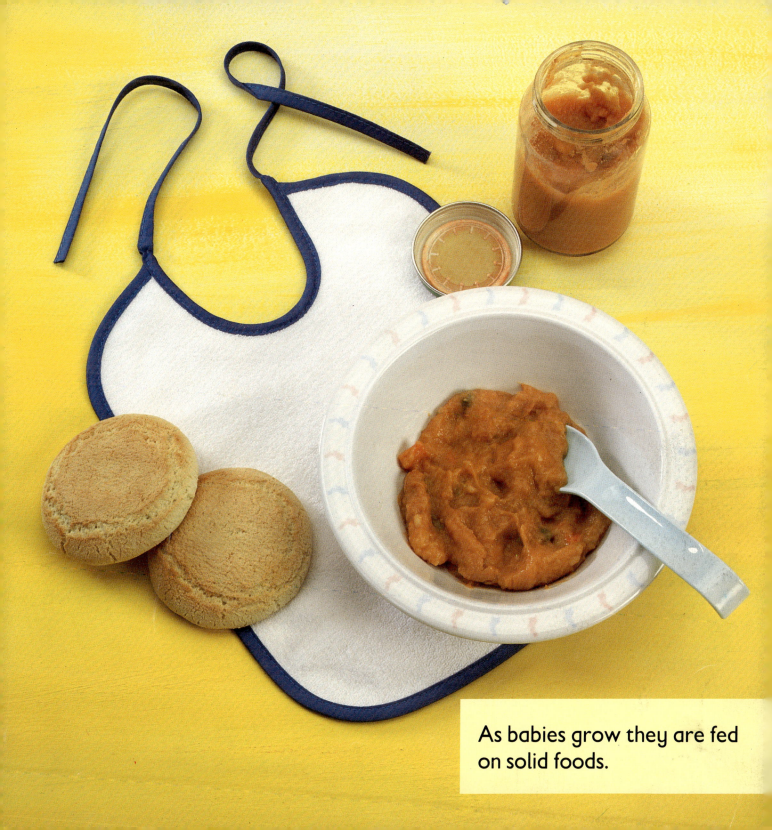

As babies grow they are fed on solid foods.

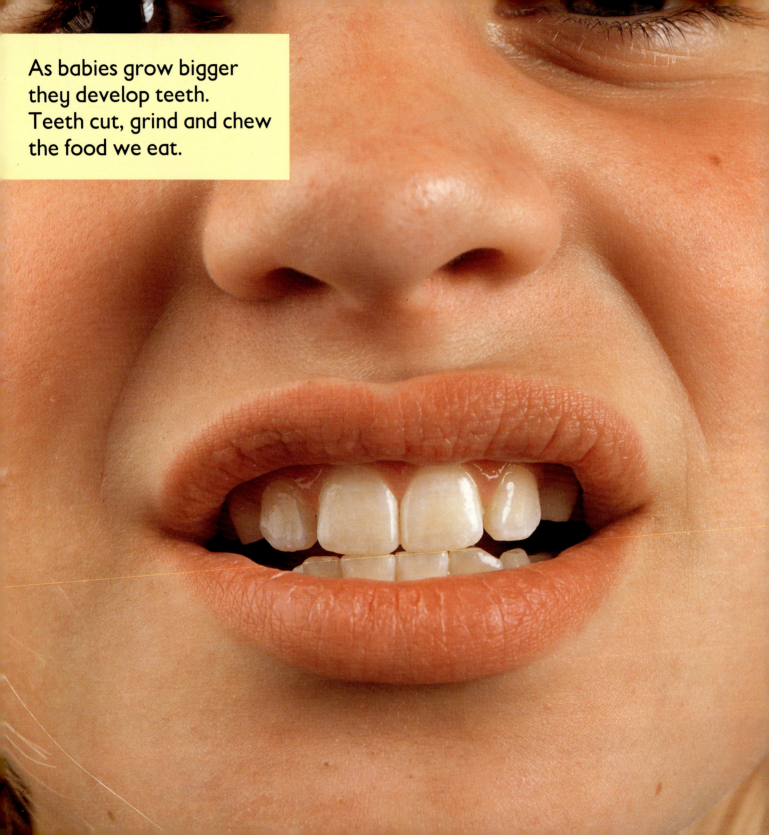

As babies grow bigger
they develop teeth.
Teeth cut, grind and chew
the food we eat.

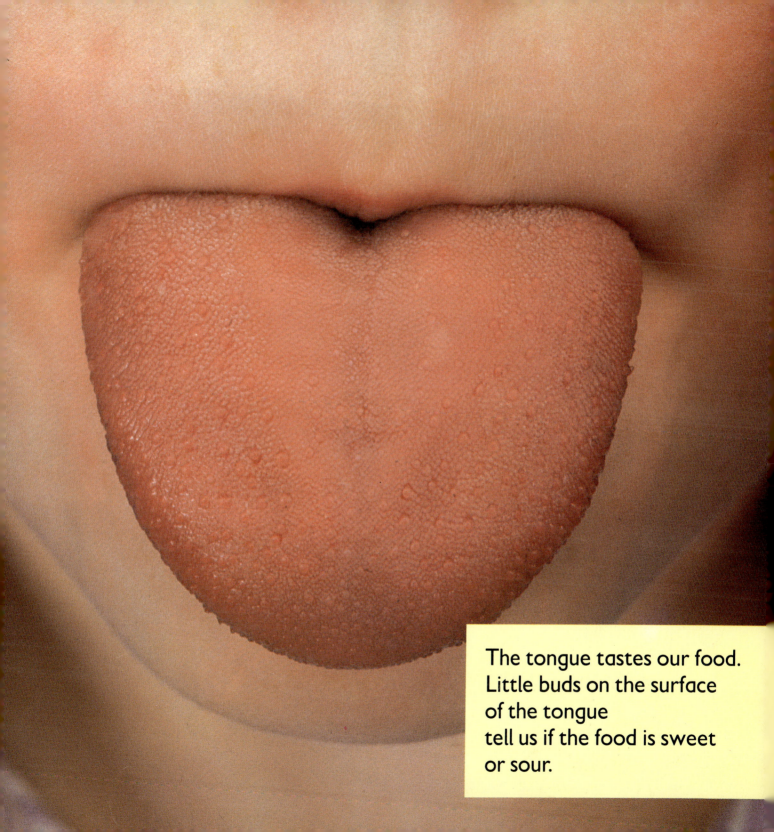

The tongue tastes our food.
Little buds on the surface
of the tongue
tell us if the food is sweet
or sour.

The food we eat is digested
in our stomach and intestines.
We are able to digest
many kinds of food.
We eat bread, potatoes
and rice.

We eat many different vegetables, fruits and nuts.

We eat meat and fish.

We eat butter, yoghurt and cheese
made from the milk of
cows, goats and sheep.

Some food we eat raw...

but some food
needs to be cooked.

We can cook food by boiling it,

baking it in an oven,

frying it in oil

or by heating it
in a microwave oven.

Some food is prepared so that it will stay fresh for many months. Food is frozen,

preserved in jars,

put in sealed cans

or cooked and stored in airtight boxes and packets. Are tins and jars airtight too?

Not everybody eats the same
kind of food.
In some parts of the world
rice is eaten
with almost every meal...

but even rice can be served
in many different ways.

Some of the foods we enjoy may not be good for us. Fried burgers and chips contain much more fat...

than a plate of cheese and salad.
Although we need to
eat some fat,
too much fat is bad for us.

Food gives us energy.
Our body uses energy
to keep warm.
Hot food helps us to feel warm
in cold weather.

But all food helps our body
to produce heat...
even ice cream
and fruit salad.

In some parts of the world the shops are full of food of all kinds.

In other parts of the world there is hunger and famine. What must it be like to live in a land of no food?

About this book

All books which are specially prepared for young children are written to meet the interest of the age group at which they are directed. This may mean presenting an idea in a humorous or unconventional way so that ideas which hitherto have been grasped somewhat hazily are given sharper focus. The books in this series aim to bring into focus some of the elements of life and living which we as adults tend to take for granted.

This book develops and explores an idea using simple text and thought-provoking photographs. The words will encourage questioning and discussion – whether they are read by adult or child. Children enjoy having information books read to them just as much as stories and poetry. The younger child may ignore the written words…pictures play an important part in learning, particularly if they encourage talk and visual discrimination.

Young children acquire much information in an incidental, almost random fashion. Indeed, they learn much just by being alive! The adult who uses books like this one needs to be sympathetic and understanding of the young child's intellectual development. It offers a particular way of looking, an approach to questioning which will result in talk, rather than "correct" one word answers.

Henry Pluckrose